# Spotlight on
# Wild Animals

**Neil Murray**

Illustrated by John Beswick, Don Forrest
David Nockels, A. Oxenham, David Pratt
and Peter Warner

HAMLYN
LONDON . NEW YORK . SYDNEY . TORONTO

# Introduction

This book is restricted to the mammals – those animals that suckle their young. Although the mammals constitute only a small part of the entire animal kingdom, there are nevertheless more than 4,000 living species – far too many for adequate discussion in a single work. The aim of this book is therefore to serve as a brief introduction to the fascinating world of mammals, and by stimulating the reader's interest, to encourage him to delve deeper into the subject.

The book is designed around the nineteen orders which form the basis of the standard method of classifying the mammals. Examples are given of species belonging to each order, as an indication of the different kinds of animals that are included in each of the main groups, which together make up the great variety of wild animals all over the world – on land, on sea, and in the air.

## Monotremes

The monotremes are the most primitive order of mammals. They are found only on the Australian mainland, in Tasmania and in New Guinea. Their ancestors broke away from the evolutionary mainstream in the early stages of mammalian development, so early in fact that they have retained a number of reptilian characteristics, both in their body structure and in their reproductive habits: they are the only mammals to lay eggs, and the males are equipped with poison spurs on the hind legs.

The living monotremes are represented by the echidnas or spiny anteaters, and by the duck-billed platypus, which is to be found only in eastern Australia and Tasmania.

**Above and below:** Echidna

This Book Belongs to
Alec MacDonald

The female echidna lays a single egg which she deposits in a small pouch on her abdomen into which milk is secreted from the mammary glands. The female platypus, on the other hand, has no pouch; she is therefore obliged to incubate the pair of eggs which form her normal clutch. To do this, she isolates herself in the underground burrow which she builds for the purpose deep into the stream bank, and envelops the eggs with her body, the process of incubation taking about a fortnight.

**Above:** The echidna's hind foot has a claw long enough to scratch between its spines

**Above and right:** Duck-billed platypus. The female has no nipples: milk oozes through pores in her skin

The platypus is largely aquatic in habit, and, like most aquatic mammals, is covered with very thick fur. It is also web-footed, and its tail is flattened like a beaver's. Its most remarkable feature, however, is the large rubbery bill which it uses to root in the muddy beds of rivers in its constant search for the worms, tadpoles and other aquatic creatures on which it feeds.

The echidna is also enveloped in fur, but with the difference that the fur contains protruding spines which provide the animal with a means of defence. If attacked, the echidna rolls itself into a ball in the same manner as a hedgehog, thus presenting a deterrent pin-cushion of spines to its attacker. A further means of defence is provided by powerful claws which also enable the echidna to dig with astonishing speed; it can quickly lower itself into the ground until only its spines are visible.

The main purpose of the claws is to assist the echidna in obtaining the termites, ants and other insects which form its main food. This diet necessitates special bodily adaptations which are very similar to those of other ant-eating mammals living on other continents. The echidna has no teeth, since it does not need them; but it has a tubular snout and an immensely long tongue. This is thickly coated with a sticky substance which forms the perfect instrument for collecting quantities of ants.

# Marsupials

At a somewhat higher evolutionary level than the monotremes are the marsupials, a name derived from the word *marsupium*, meaning 'pouch'. The young are born when they are only partly developed, and are then transferred to a pouch on the mother's stomach, where they remain until they are fully developed.

The marsupials are mainly found in Australia, Tasmania, New Guinea and Celebes; but some live in South and Central America. Their existence on two widely separated continents naturally raises the question of how such a situation came about. Several alternative solutions have been suggested, but the theory now most generally accepted is that Australia and South America once formed part of a single southern continent which separated and gradually drifted apart.

In South America there was competition from more advanced animals, which explains why only two marsupial families – the opossums and the rat opossums – have managed to survive. In Australia, on the other hand, the absence of competition – except from the dingo introduced by the early aborigines – enabled the comparatively unintelligent marsupials to flourish for millions of years. Since the end of the eighteenth century, however, Australia's native marsupials have been subjected to increasing competition from higher species of animals

**Above**: American opossum with young

**Above right**: Short-nosed bandicoot

**Above**: Long-nosed bandicoot

brought into the country from Europe and elsewhere. Competition from introduced sheep and the rabbit (which quickly became a major pest) has been particularly severe on the grass-eating marsupials. The introduction of the red fox, dogs, cats and other predatory animals such as stoats, weasels and ferrets which were set loose in a vain attempt to control the plague of rabbits, has resulted in many of the smaller native marsupials becoming scarce.

One of the most fascinating aspects of evolutionary development is the way in which the
Australian marsupials, lacking competition
from more advanced animals and with an
entire continent for their exclusive use, have
occupied all the different types of habitat that
are available in exactly the same way as
animals on other continents; not only have they
developed along parallel lines but in the process
have come to resemble some completely unrelated animals exploiting similar opportunities
elsewhere. This phenomenon, known as 'evolutionary convergence', has given rise to marsupial 'mice' which look and behave like
rodents, marsupial 'cats' which prey on smaller
marsupials and birds, a marsupial 'wolf' which
bears a striking resemblance to the wolf of the
Northern Hemisphere, and a marsupial 'mole'

**Below**: Marsupial mole

similar in appearance and habit to the African
golden mole. The wombat is a burrowing animal
with habits similar to those of the badger, and
the numbat is the marsupial equivalent of
the anteater. There are even flying phalangers,
or 'gliders' as they are popularly called, which
look very like flying squirrels; they are members

5

**Left:** Wombat

**Below left:** Sandy wallaby

**Below:** Black-gloved wallaby

of the possum family with well-developed membranes on either side of their bodies which open rather like primitive wings when they spread their limbs. This device enables the animal to launch itself into space and glide from tree to tree.

The best-known marsupials are, of course, the many kinds of kangaroos and wallabies, ranging from rat-kangaroos the size of rabbits to the red, or plains, kangaroo, the largest living marsupial: an adult male can stand more than 7 feet tall. The red kangaroo's arms are small and weak, but its legs are immensely powerful. They are used to propel the animal over the ground in a series of gigantic leaps, each covering about 20-25 feet, at the speed of a racehorse. Some kangaroos have taken to living in the trees: unlike their ground-dwelling relatives, the tree-kangaroos have well-developed arms to assist them in climbing and grasping branches.

**Above:** Long-nosed rat-kangaroo, or potoroo

**Above:** Leadbeater's possum

One of the most interesting tree-dwelling marsupials is the koala which inhabits the eucalypt forests of eastern Australia. The koala has very particular tastes; its diet consists exclusively of the leaves of certain species of eucalypts at a certain stage of growth. It never drinks, but obtains all its liquid requirements from its leafy food. Koala females bear only a single young. Between leaving the pouch at the age of about 6 months and being weaned at 12 months, the young koala is carried on its mother's back.

Among the most exciting zoological events of recent years has been the rediscovery of several species of marsupial which were thought to be extinct. These include Leadbeater's possum, the scaly-tailed possum, and a primitive phalanger with the scientific name of *Burramys parvus* which had previously been known only from jaw and other bone fragments found in owl-pellet deposits.

**Right:** Koala bear and young

# Insectivores

The insectivores are the most primitive of the more advanced animals. They are small, rather unintelligent animals, with poor eyesight, and feed mainly on insects, worms and other small creatures. But despite being slow-witted, they have spread widely throughout every continent except for Australasia, South America and the Arctic regions.

This order is made up of eight families, by far the largest being the shrews. Despite their tiny size – most shrews are less than 3 inches long – they are extraordinarily ferocious and do not hesitate to attack animals far bigger than themselves. They are assisted by having poisonous saliva, which helps to paralyze their prey.

**Above:** Long-eared desert hedgehog

**Below:** Otter shrew

Some insectivores have become adapted to living in water. Among them are several species of water shrews which live in the rivers of Europe, Asia and America. Another aquatic insectivore is the desman, a web-footed member of the mole family. One species of desman lives in Russia and another in the Pyrenees. They are the only surviving representatives of a once much larger group of animals. They owe their survival to their way of life which is so highly specialized – they live in cold, fast-flowing rivers – that they compete with no other animal and none competes with them. The only threat to their survival arises from the possibility of river pollution and the construction of dams for hydro-electric purposes.

Yet another interesting aquatic insectivore is the otter shrew, of which there are three species, all inhabiting tropical Africa. One of them attains a length of more than 2 feet, and is the largest living insectivore. In general appearance it looks something like an otter, and is equally at home in the water.

Two insectivore families, comprising the hedgehogs and the tenrecs, have followed the echidna in developing spines on their bodies as a means of protection. The hedgehogs are common animals of Europe, Asia and Africa, but the tenrecs are found only in Madagascar. Some tenrecs are coloured bright yellow and black as a warning to potential enemies, and have detachable spines on their heads and bodies which they thrust into any attacker. One of the tenrecs, *Limnogale,* has become aquatic, in the course of which it has developed

webbed hind feet: it feeds on insect larvae, freshwater shrimps, and small frogs. Another, *Microgale dobsoni*, stores fat in its tail when insect food is abundant, thus establishing a reserve supply on which it can draw in times of scarcity. In this it resembles a marsupial, the fat-tailed sminthopsis, and several other unrelated animals. The tenrecs have been little studied, and much remains to be learned about them.

The islands of Cuba and Haiti are the only places in the world to possess the remarkable solenodon. These rat-sized insectivores have a long snout, large claws, and special glands which give off a musky smell. Solenodons have become rare as the result of spreading cultivation which is destroying the native forest in which they live.

**Right**: Solenodon

# 'Flying lemurs'

This order is made up of only a single family comprising two rather similar species, one ranging quite widely through South East Asia and Indonesia from Burma to Java, and the other inhabiting the Philippines.

The commonly accepted name 'flying lemur' is in fact misleading, for although these animals have heads and faces which bear a slight resemblance to some of the lemurs of Madagascar, they are in no way related. Moreover, they do not fly in the manner of birds or bats, for they have no real wings. Instead, they have a flap of skin on either side of the body extending from neck to wrist to ankle, and from ankle to tail; this normally hangs loosely about them like a cloak, but becomes fully extended when the animal stretches out its arms and legs, thus acting as a simple fixed wing. This primitive method of flight enables the animal to cover a considerable distance, but its scope is strictly limited for the line of flight is always downwards. It cannot be compared with the soaring flight of a bird. Before launching itself into space, the flying lemur must first attain height. To help it climb the trunks and branches of trees it is provided with sharp claws on hands and feet with which to grip the bark. Flying lemurs seldom descend to the ground and when they do they cannot stand on their limbs but crawl in an ungainly manner – an extreme example of an animal that has become so adapted to its highly specialized way of life that its arms and legs can no longer be used in the ordinary way. This also explains why the flying lemur spends most of the time hanging upside-down in preference to what we would regard as the right way up.

Flying lemurs live in the trees searching for the leaves, seeds and fruit on which they feed. They are not active during the day, spending most of the time either in a hole in a tree or suspended from a branch, and as the brownish coloration of their coat blends so well with the bark they are difficult to see. Their nocturnal existence helps to explain why so little is known about them.

Adult females normally bear only a single young which is usually left hanging from a branch while its mother moves about searching for food, but it occasionally accompanies her by clinging to her fur.

**Above**: Flying lemur

# Bats

Bats form the second largest order of mammals; only the rodent order has a greater number of species. There are almost a thousand species of bats, and they are widely distributed on every continent. The only extensive areas from which they are absent are the Arctic and Antarctic regions.

Bats are the only mammals capable of true flight in the manner of a bird: some have even adopted the practice of migrating like birds to avoid the cold of winter. The power of flight has been achieved by fundamental changes in the body structure, notably by a lengthening of the arms, and in particular of the fingers, the bones of which have become almost as long as the body to provide the necessary 'struts' supporting the wing membrane. In many species the thumb projects from the leading edge of the wing, its tip equipped with a hooked claw.

Their ability to fly has resulted in bats being the only land mammals to have colonized many oceanic islands; though some islands are so remote that even bats have been unable to reach them. Two species of bats are the only native mammals inhabiting New Zealand: all New Zealand's other mammals were introduced by man.

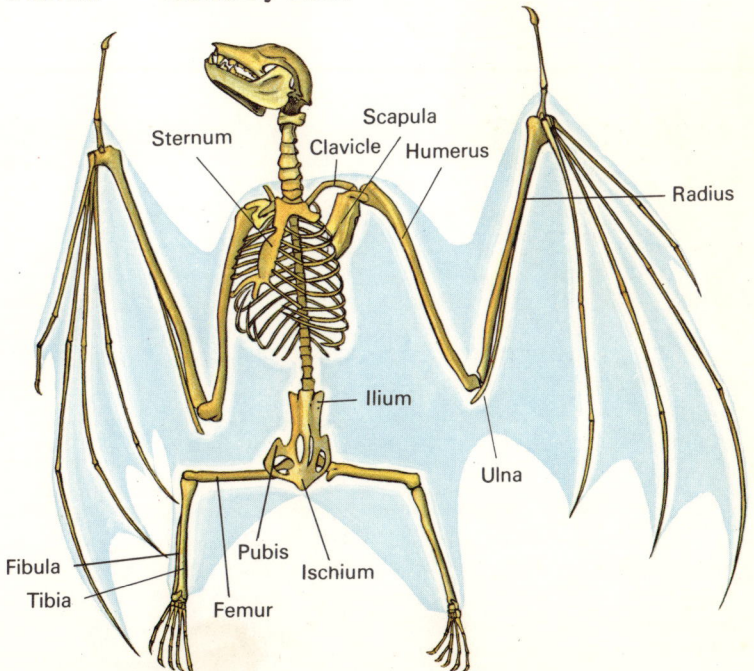

**Above**: Fruit bat, or 'flying fox'

**Right**: Skeleton of a fruit bat

Scapula
Sternum
Clavicle
Humerus
Radius
Ilium
Ulna
Fibula
Tibia
Pubis
Ischium
Femur

The bats are divided into two basic branches, or suborders: those that eat fruit and those that eat insects. The fruit bats, or 'flying foxes' as they are usually called, are comparatively large, besides possessing good eyesight and a keen sense of smell. They spend the day roosting in caves, rock crevices, hollow trees, or among the branches and foliage, where they hang upside-down, emerging at dusk to feed. A colony of these bats descending on an orchard and gorging itself on fruit can inflict considerable damage, so it is easy to see that they are not popular with fruit farmers.

**Above**: Little brown bat

**Left**: Long-tongued bat

The insect-eating bats, on the other hand, are small and have poor eyesight. But they compensate for their poor vision by exceptionally sensitive hearing which has evolved into what is virtually a highly developed 'radar' system. This enables them to fly with uncanny accuracy in the dark. The built-in radar operates by the bat sending out a series of very high-pitched sounds, either through its mouth or its nostrils; these sounds are reflected back from any object they meet to the bat's large and highly-developed ears, indicating its precise position. This device is so sensitive and so accurate that a bat can move swiftly and unhesitatingly through an intricate maze of obstructions in pitch darkness without touching them; it can also detect and catch a flying insect by the same method.

**Below**: Tomb bat

**Left**: Bulldog bat

Although most insectivorous bats live exclusively on insects, some have acquired a taste for nectar or pollen, and have developed extremely long tongues to reach into flowers. In the process they have come to perform an important rôle in the pollination of certain flowers. Others have become flesh-eaters, devouring small rodents, reptiles and birds. The bulldog bat has taken to fishing, catching small fish with its clawed feet as it skims close to the surface. Some even prey on other bats. The true vampires, of

**Above**: Antillean tree bat

**Above**: Vampire bat

which there are only three species – all inhabiting Central and South America – have adopted a diet of blood. Vampires cause heavy losses to the livestock industry by spreading disease.

The strange appearance and habits of bats have caused them to be regarded by many people as objects of fear and dread, and this is reflected in the folklore of many countries. These beliefs are groundless, however, since except for the vampires, most bats are harmless.

13

# Primates

The non-human primates are widely distributed throughout the tropical regions of southern Asia, Africa, and Central and Southern America. They are divided into two main groups: the prosimians, or primitive primates, among them the lemurs, lorises, bushbabies and tarsiers, all of which are found only in the Old World; and the anthropoids, or higher primates, which include all the New World species plus a number from the Old World.

**Below left:** Ring-tailed lemur
**Below right:** Ruffed lemur

Madagascar is the only place in the world now inhabited by lemurs. These primitive primates were at one time more widely distributed, but were replaced by the more advanced monkeys. They owe their survival in Madagascar to the fact that the island became separated from the African mainland before the monkeys had evolved. For millions of years, therefore, long after the lemurs had disappeared elsewhere, they remained in Madagascar, cut off from contact – and thus from competition – with higher primates. Madagascar's long isolation has resulted in the island becoming an evolutionary backwater, which explains why zoologists and botanists regard it as of such exceptional interest and importance.

The lemurs and their allies vary in size from the little mouse lemurs which fit easily into the

**Above:** Tarsier

palm of one's hand, to the ruffed lemur and the indris, which are more than 3 feet tall. Both these large animals are regarded by the local people as sun-worshippers because of their habit of greeting the dawn with widespread arms. It was for this reason that they were until recently regarded as sacred. The indris has an extraordinarily powerful voice: when it gives tongue, its cry rolls through the forest in a great wave of sound.

One of the most common species is the ring-tailed lemur. It has a very distinctively marked black and white tail which it frequently runs through its arms, in the process daubing it with scent from special glands on its wrists. The scented tail is then erected vertically above its body; and the manner in which it is waved shows other lemurs the animal's mood.

**Above left:** Verreaux's sifaka
**Above right:** Indris

**Below:** Aye-aye

One of the rarest and most interesting of all Madagascar's primates is the aye-aye, which is estimated to have been reduced to fewer than 50 individual animals. Some of the surviving aye-ayes have been transferred to an uninhabited island off the coast of Madagascar in an attempt to save the species from extinction.

The marmosets and tamarins, of which there are more than fifty species, are inhabitants of the Amazonian forests. All are small, the smallest being the pygmy marmoset whose body is only 4 inches long. They are attractive little creatures with long tails and shrill, bird-like voices. Some have long manes. They live in small family groups, feeding on vegetation, fruit, insects, and sometimes birds.

**Above:** Emperor tamarin

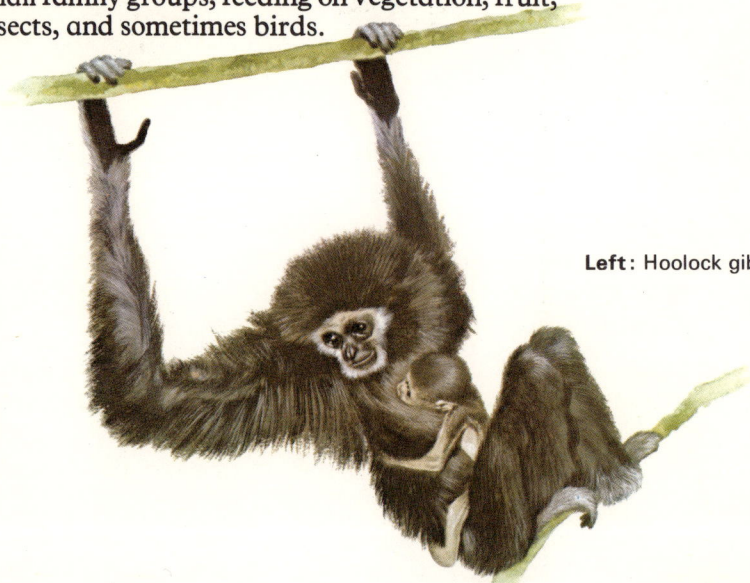

**Left:** Hoolock gibbon and young

The Amazon region is also the home of three species of uakaris. The red uakari is distinguished by a face that is permanently bright scarlet, and all three species become flushed when disturbed or annoyed. The long chestnut coloured hair covering their bodies contrasts strongly with their bald heads.

The most common of the New World monkeys are the squirrel monkeys, capuchins, and spider monkeys. The spider monkeys have slender bodies and very long arms – longer than their legs – which they use to swing beneath the branches in much the same manner as a gibbon. They are also provided with an extremely powerful tail; this acts as a fifth limb, for it is strong enough to bear the animal's full weight. The closely related woolly monkeys, as their name suggests, are covered with a woolly coat.

**Below:** De Brazza's monkey

**Below:** Male gorilla

Most primates are forest dwellers. The various species have adapted themselves to living at different levels in the forest. Some, such as the red colobus, live in the topmost branches of the trees and seldom descend. The black and white colobus, on the other hand, prefers the lower strata. Others, such as the strikingly coloured mandrill, choose to live on the forest floor. Several species, notably the baboon, the patas, and the vervet monkey, have forsaken the forest altogether and moved on to the grasslands, though at night they still return to the security of the trees.

Excluding man, the most advanced and intelligent of the primates are the orang-utan, chimpanzee and gorilla, known collectively as the Great Apes. Their immense size obliges them to spend most of the time on the ground, but they retire to the trees to sleep, constructing primitive 'nests' of branches and foliage in which they spend the night.

**Left:** Preuss's monkey

**Right:** White-throated guenon

17

# Edentates

The edentates are an order of mammals that is found only in Central and South America, except for a single species – the nine-banded armadillo – which has spread into the southern part of the United States.

The order is divided into three distinctive families, the anteaters, sloths and armadillos. All are small-brained, unintelligent animals which evolved when South America was an isolated island continent, and it is surprising that they have managed to survive subsequent competition from animals more advanced than themselves. Some of their predecessors, however, were not so successful: these included giant ground sloths, or megatheres, standing more than 16 feet tall, which may have existed until after the coming of early man; and extinct relatives of the present-day armadillos, called glyptodonts, which were 6 feet long and wholly encased in heavy armour that made them safe from virtually all attacks.

**Above:** Giant anteater

Three of the four living species of anteaters are small and live in dense forests. One, the dwarf anteater, spends its life permanently high up in the trees, but the fourth, the giant anteater, lives in more open country and grasslands. The appearance of the giant anteater is most extraordinary, for it is designed for a highly specialized existence. Its overall length is about 6 feet from nose to tip of tail. Its most noticeable feature is an exceptionally long tube-like snout through which an immensely long tongue emerges from a toothless mouth; special glands keep the tongue permanently coated with a sticky substance. After using its powerful claws to break into a termites' nest, the anteater thrusts its tongue deep into the galleries of the nest licking up large numbers of the occupants.

The seven species of sloths are all forest dwellers. They spend their lives in the trees in constant but leisurely search for the leaves, fruit and other vegetation that forms their diet, moving very slowly upside-down beneath the branches from which they suspend themselves by massive hook-like claws. Their long ragged coats are usually covered with algae which give them a greenish appearance.

The armadillos, of which there are more than twenty species, range in size from the 5 foot long giant armadillo weighing more than 100 pounds to the tiny fairy armadillo, or lesser pichiciego, which is less than 6 inches long. All are expert diggers living in underground burrows, who roll themselves into balls when attacked.

The giant armadillo is covered with tough body armour. It also has the distinction of

**Above left**: Two-toed sloth
**Above**: Dwarf anteater

**Below**: Three-banded armadillos roll themselves into balls when threatened

possessing on each of its fore-limbs an immense claw, larger than that of any other mammal. This powerful tool is used for ripping open the nests of the ants, termites and other insects on which it feeds; the claw is also used for defence, and to enable the animal to burrow even into the hardest soils at incredible speed.

**Above**: Giant armadillo

Despite its small size, the fairy armadillo can dig almost equally rapidly. This little animal is only partly armoured: it has a series of about twenty pink horny plates reaching across its back from head to rump and lying at right angles to the spine to which they are attached. The rump plate, through which the tail protrudes, is welded to the pelvis. Beneath the plates the body is covered with long silky hairs. The fairy armadillo spends most of its time below the ground and is rarely seen on the surface. Its method of defence is to withdraw its tail into its rump plate and present its armoured rear to its assailant, at the same time wedging itself firmly against the walls of its burrow.

**Right**: Fairy armadillo

# Pangolins

The pangolins, or scaly anteaters as they are sometimes called, consist of seven closely related species which are distributed through tropical Africa, India, South East Asia and Indonesia.

The upper part of the pangolin's body is covered with a series of overlapping armoured scales resembling those of a reptile but, like rhinoceros horn, made of compressed hair. The underside is covered with normal hair. When attacked, the pangolin rolls itself into a ball in the manner of a hedgehog or armadillo thus protecting its vulnerable underparts.

Its head is small, its snout elongated, its tongue long, its mouth toothless, its claws powerful digging tools. In all these respects and in their shape and general appearance the pangolins look something like the anteaters of South America, but are in no way related. This is a further example of parallel development of unrelated species mentioned on page 5, for although pangolins and anteaters have evolved quite separately on different continents, they have developed along similar lines.

Like the anteaters, some of the species of pangolins live on the ground and others in the trees. The tree-dwelling pangolins have developed long tails which they use to help grasp branches or tree trunks as they move about. The tail is also used as an additional support when the animal either walks on its hind legs or sits, thus leaving the hands free. Pangolins are seldom seen as they spend the day in their burrows, emerging only at night to search for the termites and ants on which they feed.

**Above**: Tree pangolin

**Left**: Temminck's pangolin

# Lagomorphs

The distribution of the lagomorphs covers almost the entire world: the only areas in which they are not naturally represented are the Antarctic and Australasia. As already mentioned in discussing the marsupials, rabbits have, however, been artificially introduced into Australia with devastating consequences.

The order is divided into two families, one containing the rabbits and hares, and the other the much smaller pikas or conies.

Rabbits and hares are creatures of the open grasslands. As a family they can tolerate a wide range of climatic conditions, from the cold winters of temperate Europe, Asia and North America to tropical heat and near-desert conditions.

**Right**: Pikas

Pikas, on the other hand, are confined to the higher and colder parts of Asia and North America. The American pikas are found only in the Rocky Mountains and parts of Alaska and the Yukon. They meet the problem of surviving the harsh winters in much the same way as many farmers: during the summer, when fresh vegetation is plentiful, they cut and gather a crop of green food; after leaving it to dry in the sun, they stack the hay in some protected spot ready for winter feed.

Rabbits live in warrens formed of a maze of burrows tunnelled into the ground. They are notoriously prolific breeders; females mature early and give birth to a litter of 4-6 young after only 29 days gestation, mating again almost immediately, thus producing several litters a year.

Hares are bigger than rabbits, with longer legs and bigger ears. They also differ in habit:

in contrast to rabbits which flee to their burrows when alarmed, hares instinctively 'freeze' to the ground in the hope that the danger will pass them by. Only if that ruse fails will they run. They then run strongly, dodging and changing course frequently to throw off pursuit. Instead of living underground like rabbits, they occupy 'forms' – shallow depressions – on the surface. The leverets, as young hares are called, are much more developed at birth than rabbits, they are covered with fur and have their eyes fully open. Young leverets do not remain long with their mother but disperse singly over a wide area. Apart from periodical visits from their mother for feeding, they remain on their own. In this way the chances of an entire litter being wiped out are greatly reduced. Furthermore, leverets have no scent; this, coupled with their instinct to remain absolutely motionless when danger threatens, means that a marauding dog or other predator can pass very close without realizing the leveret is there.

**Below**: Arctic hares

# Rodents

This order of mammals contains a larger number of species than any other: it is also the most numerous in terms of individual animals. Although they vary greatly in general appearance and habit, all rodents have sharp, constantly growing incisor teeth in both the upper and lower jaws which are specially designed for gnawing, and cheek teeth for grinding the different kinds of vegetation on which they feed. The rodent order has three broad subdivisions: the squirrels and their relatives; the rats and mice; and the porcupines and their allies.

Almost without exception, the rodents are small-bodied animals. The largest is the capybara of Central and South America, which is about 4 feet long and weighs more than 100 pounds. But what they lack in size they make up in numbers, for rodents are prolific breeders. They are also highly adaptable; their ability to live under such a wide range of conditions has enabled them to spread almost everywhere throughout the world, from snow-covered regions to the hottest deserts.

**Above**: Capybara

**Right**: Mouse

**Below**: Dusky field rat

**Below**: Brown mouse

Rats and mice have been particularly enterprising in this respect, to the extent that they can be regarded as among the most successful animals that have ever lived. By their close association with man, rats and mice have even colonized continents and islands in which they do not naturally occur, for they were uninvited passengers aboard the ships of the early explorers and navigators. The arrival of these aggressive stowaways invariably had disastrous effects on the native animals which were

**Above**: Eastern pseudo-rat

24

usually incapable of offering any resistance. Island faunas have suffered particularly severely from introduced rats: the eggs of ground-nesting birds, turtles and tortoises are especially vulnerable to them. Rats are also responsible for the spreading of disease, not only to other animals but to human beings as well. The Black Death, for example, which devastated Europe in the Middle Ages, was carried by rats. Within a period of five years (1347–52) this plague killed more than a third of all the people in Europe.

During the course of evolution the rodents have taken advantage of every possible opportunity for living that different types of environment can offer. Most rodents live in burrows but spend much of their time on the surface searching for food, dashing back to the safety of their burrow at the first hint of danger. An exception is the mara, or Patagonian cavy, which looks very like a hare and relies on speed

to escape its enemies. The porcupines have adopted yet another method of defence: by raising the spines along their backs they present a formidable pin-cushion to any animal rash enough to attack them. The mole rats on the other hand (one species of which is practically hairless), live permanently underground. Some rodents have climbed up into the trees; some have become fliers; others have taken to the water.

Of the many burrowing rodents, the prairie dog – so-called because its cry resembles a bark – is one of the most engaging. When settlers from Europe first arrived in North America, the open grasslands of the Great Plains were covered with prairie dog 'towns' and 'cities', the popular names for the extensive systems of underground burrows in which the immense colonies of prairie dogs lived. When the plains were developed for cattle ranching the prairie dog became unpopular with the ranchers who wanted the land and grazing for their cattle. Measures were therefore taken to reduce the prairie dog population.

**Above**: Prairie dogs

**Below**: Red squirrel

**Below left**: Horsefield's flying squirrel

**Centre**: Eastern flying squirrel

The squirrels are among the most skilful climbing rodents; they are found in almost every part of the world except Australasia and Antarctica. They spend much of their time busily engaged in ceaseless search for the nuts, fruit and berries on which they feed. When summer ends, squirrels establish hoards of food in convenient places to see them through the winter. The red squirrel, once so familiar in English woodlands, has been largely driven out by the introduced grey squirrel.

Most of the flying squirrels live in Asia, though two species inhabit North America and one reaches into eastern Europe. They have flaps of skin on either side of their bodies similar to the gliding membranes of the 'gliders' and flying lemurs already mentioned. This device is invaluable both as a means of enabling them to escape their enemies and as an aid in their continuous search for food.

Apart from the water vole, coypu and various species of water rats, the best known examples of rodents that have taken to water are the beaver and muskrat. Both are covered with highly valued fur, which is why they have long been hunted. The beaver, one of the largest of the rodents, has a broad, flat tail like a paddle which is of great assistance in swimming. Beavers construct complex systems of dams linked by canals as a means of maintaining a constant level of water around the 'lodges' in which they live. The trees and branches used to construct the dam walls are gnawed into convenient lengths and carried to the site.

**Above:** Mountain beaver

**Above and left:** Jerboa

One of the most attractive rodents is the jerboa, of which there are about twenty-five species; most of them live in Asia, but three species are found in North Africa. The jerboa is a small, sand-coloured animal with a long tufted tail, large eyes and ears, tiny arms and outsize hind feet. This little animal stands only a few inches tall, yet it can leap three yards in a single bound. Jerboas spend the day beneath the ground to avoid the great heat of the deserts in which they live, coming to the surface only at night when its is cool.

# Cetaceans

The cetaceans are an order of mammals that has moved from the land to the sea. In the process of evolution their bodies have become modified to living permanently in water: their hind legs have disappeared, their arms have changed into flippers, and their tails have become flattened. Their hair has completely vanished except for a few bristles on the chin and snout: its function in keeping the body warm has been taken by a thick layer of blubber beneath the smooth skin. The external ears have vanished, and the nostrils have been replaced by either a single or double blow-hole on top of the head.

There are two main groups of cetaceans: the toothed whales and the whalebone whales. The toothed whales include all the dolphins and porpoises; they feed on fish and other marine animals. The whalebone whales, on the other hand, feed on plankton – small marine organisms which exist in vast numbers. Instead of teeth, these whales have a series of horny plates hanging from the roof of the mouth, each of which is covered with bristle-like fibres acting as a sieve. When feeding, the whale swims through the concentrations of plankton with its huge mouth wide open. On closing its jaws and pressing its tongue upwards against

**Above**: Sperm whale

**Left**: Geoffroy's dolphin

**Below**: Porpoise

the roof of its mouth, the incoming water is strained through the plates and out of the sides of the mouth, leaving a mass of plankton behind.

The whalebone whales include the blue whale, the largest animal that has ever lived – larger even than the huge dinosaurs that dominated the earth many millions of years ago. An adult blue whale may be 100 feet long and weigh

28

as much as 160 tons. Newborn calves are 23 feet long and weigh more than two tons; they are said to consume more than half a ton of milk a day. Animals of such gigantic size could only evolve in the oceans where the water can support their huge bodies.

Unlike the seals and other marine mammals which breed on land, the cetaceans spend all their lives in water. Births take place at sea, the mother assisting the new-born calf to the surface to take its first breath, for, like all other mammals, whales draw their oxygen from the air and must therefore surface at regular intervals to breath. Even so, they can remain submerged for considerable periods.

Whales are found in all the world's oceans. Many species undertake lengthy seasonal migrations, spending the summer in the vicinity of the pack ice where plankton is particularly abundant, and moving into equatorial waters to avoid the polar winter and to give birth in a warm climate, for whale calves are born without a thick layer of blubber to keep them warm.

**Below**: Blue whale

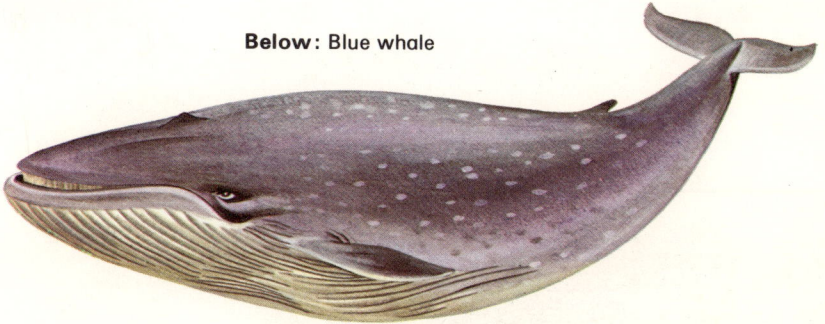

Cetaceans, and particularly dolphins, are very sociable animals, living together in 'schools', some of which are very large. They have an extremely high level of intelligence, and can be trained to perform a variety of complicated tasks, including carrying items of equipment from the surface to skin-divers working on the sea bed. They communicate with each other by means of a series of high-pitched sounds – a particularly useful method of maintaining contact in the vast expanses of the ocean.

Not all dolphins live in the sea; four species of river dolphins and the Amazonian white dolphin have adapted themselves to living in some of the larger river systems, including the Ganges, the Yangtse and the Amazon.

# Carnivores

Carnivores are flesh-eating animals equipped with large and efficient teeth set in powerful jaws. The order is represented in every part of the world except Australia and New Zealand; even there, several species have been artificially introduced by man.

The carnivores are divided into seven principal groups: the dog family; the bears; the raccoons and their relatives; the otters, badgers, skunks and weasels; the genets, mongooses and their allies; the hyenas; and the cats.

Of the seven species of bears, the brown bear is the most widely distributed: its range includes North America, northern and central Asia and eastern Europe. A few small groups still survive in western Europe. Brown bears vary greatly in size and colour, from the small sandy-coloured specimens of the Middle East to the dark Alaskan grizzlies, among them the huge Kodiak bear, the largest living carnivore, which may weigh more than a ton.

**Below**: Brown bear

**Right**: Tiger

The striped hyena is a flesh-eater that has become adapted to devouring carrion. It is one of nature's dustmen, sharing with jackals and vultures the important task of keeping the countryside clean and healthy. Hyenas can often be seen lurking at a respectful distance from a lion's kill waiting for the pride of lions to leave so that they can move in to finish the remains.

Although a much smaller animal, the aardwolf bears a striking resemblance to the striped hyena and is frequently mistaken for one. The two animals are related, but the aardwolf's way of life is entirely different: it feeds on termites and other insects, and its teeth have become adapted to this particular function.

The cat family contains thirty-six species, ranging from the wild cat which is little bigger than an ordinary domestic cat, to the tiger,

**Below**: Raccoon
**Bottom**: Marten

**Above**: Snow leopard

the largest of which can weigh more than 600 pounds. The tiger has a very wide distribution from Iran to Siberia and Manchuria, and from India to Indonesia, but is now rare almost everywhere.

The range of the leopard is even greater, for it is found not only over much of Asia but in Africa also. Its near relative, the snow leopard, lives on the cold highland steppes of Central Asia, following the seasonal movements of the wild sheep and other animals on which it preys:

31

it spends the summer on the open alpine grasslands at heights of up to 18,000 feet and descends lower into the valleys as winter approaches. Like its relative, the clouded leopard of South East Asia and Indonesia, it is very rare and seldom seen.

In South America the place of the leopard is taken by the jaguar, the largest of the American wild cats, which ranges from Central America to northern Patagonia. It is primarily an animal of the lowland forests, but is sometimes found either at high altitude or on the open grasslands of the pampas. Although it normally hunts on land, it has no hesitation in following its prey into the water; unlike most cats, it seems to enjoy swimming.

The ocelot, like the jaguar, has a patterned coat which helps make it less conspicuous in the dense forests in which it lives. It also serves to make the pelt attractive to man: ocelot fur is so valuable that the animal is relentlessly hunted.

The South American cats include the pampas cat which is widespread in the Andean valleys

**Above**: Cheetahs

**Left**: Caracal lynx

and on lowland grasslands, and the Andean cat which inhabits the higher parts of the Andes. The Andean cat is extremely rare: only half a dozen specimens have ever been recorded.

In contrast to the forest-dwelling cats, the cheetah is an animal of the open grasslands and semi-deserts of Africa and southwestern Asia. As the open country in which it lives provides little cover for stalking, the cheetah has to rely on a sudden burst of speed to catch its quarry. It is also an unrivalled sprinter: over a short distance it can run faster than any other animal.

**Below**: Serval

The northern lynx once ranged through all the northern forests of Eurasia and North America. It remains well distributed in Asia and Canada but has disappeared from most of Europe. It is still found in parts of Scandinavia and eastern Europe, however, and has even managed to survive in Spain, where there is a distinctive subspecies. In the warmer and drier parts of Eurasia the place of the northern lynx is taken by the caracal lynx whose range extends into Africa.

**Below**: Wolf

33

# Seals

The seals are another order of mammals that has moved into the sea. They are not, however, as highly specialized for marine life as the whales and dolphins: although much of their lives is spent in the sea, they return to the land to breed, give birth and rear their young, at which time they congregate in large numbers. Some species spend several months of every year ashore. In the process of evolution their bodies have become streamlined and their

**Below**: Walrus

limbs have become flippers. These are invaluable aids to efficient swimming but make for clumsy movement ashore.

The seals are divided into three main groups: the fur seals and sealions; the walrus; and the common seals, monk seals, elephant seals and their relations. Seals of one species or another are found in almost every ocean. The greatest concentrations are in the colder seas and around the polar regions. The walruses, for example,

**Left**: Elephant seal

34

**Left**: Australian sealion

live almost entirely north of the Arctic Circle. Some seals, notably those in Lake Baikal, have been cut off from the sea and have become adapted to living in fresh water.

Seals are covered with short fur, the pelts of the fur seals being particularly valuable. When the first explorers sailed around Cape Horn and

**Below**: Australian fur seal

**Above**: Leopard seal

along the Pacific coast of South America, they found the beaches and offshore islands crowded with literally millions of fur seals. This discovery led to a period of ruthless hunting for the fur trade, which ended only when there were no longer enough seals left for hunting to be profitable.

**Right**: Sealion

35

# Aardvark

The aardvark, or antbear as it is often called, has been placed in an order of its own. In its general appearance this curious animal looks like an anteater, but is not related. It is about the size of a pig, with prominent ears, arched back and thick tail; it has an elongated snout and pig-like muzzle, with the long tongue and lack of teeth typical of an ant-eating animal. It is covered with a tough leathery skin and bristly hairs, and is equipped with powerful claws for digging and for defence.

The aardvark inhabits open country wherever there are termites in Africa south of the Sahara. It leads a solitary life, spending the day underground and emerging from its burrow only at night, which explains why it is so seldom

**Above and below**: Aardvark

seen and why so little is known about it. Its presence can usually be guessed from the presence of 'pig-holes'. In some areas these can be very numerous. Abandoned pig-holes with their entrances obscured by grass are a menace to horsemen. They are however extremely useful to a large number of wild animals, including warthogs, ground squirrels, many small carnivores, snakes, and even owls, which take up residence in them.

Although normally slow-moving on the ground, the aardvark shares with the anteater the ability to dig at astonishing speed: attempts to capture it in its burrow are seldom successful as the aardvark can burrow much faster than a team of men can dig.

# Elephants

The elephants at one time formed a large order of mammals; but of the hundreds of species that once inhabited the earth only two are alive today: the Asiatic and the African.

The Asiatic elephant lives in Ceylon, India and South East Asia. It is the smaller of the two species, with small ears, curved back, and bulbous forehead. Females of this species have no visible tusks. Asiatic elephants have long been trained in the service of man, a practice so ancient that its beginnings are older than recorded history. War-elephants were for centuries a feature of Asiatic armies, the tanks of antiquity. The elephant became a symbol of power and prestige: besides being valued for military purposes it took part in elaborate court and temple ceremonies. Even today the Asiatic elephant is widely used as a working animal, particularly in forestry.

**Above**: Indian elephant

The African elephant is the largest living land mammal, bigger than its Asiatic relative, and having immense ears and a flat forehead. Both cows and bulls have tusks, though cow ivory is smaller.

The elephant's most remarkable feature is unquestionably its trunk. This unique organ has many different functions: it is a powerful yet sensitive and highly flexible instrument, combining the functions of nose and hand: besides being used for breathing, it has strength enough to lift a tree trunk yet the delicacy to pick up a feather or to take a young bird from its nest without causing it harm. It is invaluable for gathering the vast quantities of food required by such a bulky animal, and for grasping objects that would otherwise be beyond reach, whether leaves from the higher branches of trees or water from below ground level.

Elephants are highly sociable animals, living in herds which sometimes contain many hundreds of animals. They are normally placid and tolerant, but when annoyed or disturbed they can be very aggressive, particularly cows with young calves at foot.

**Below:** African elephants

## Hyraxes

The rodent-like appearance of the hyraxes is deceptive; they have no close relatives – their nearest being the elephants and the sirenians (see page 40) – and their ancestry is obscure. They have therefore been placed in an order of their own.

The hyraxes, or dassies, are mainly confined to Africa, with an extension of range into the Arabian Peninsula northwards as far as Syria.

There are six species divided between the rock hyraxes and the tree hyraxes.

The hyrax looks something like a marmot, with short legs, and a tail so stumpy that it is practically non-existent. Its fur is thick and coarse and mingled with long bristles. In the centre of its back is a prominent patch concealing a special gland. Its feet have several unusual features including soles equipped with special rubbery pads which remain constantly moist, thereby greatly assisting the animal in gaining a foothold on smooth surfaces.

**Above:** Rock hyrax

Rock hyraxes are sociable animals. They live in crevices and hollows among the rocky outcrops which are a regular feature of the African grasslands. They spend much of the day sunning themselves, but their keen eyesight is always alert for danger, and they are quick to dash for cover at the approach of an eagle or other predator.

Tree hyraxes are inhabitants of the African forests, and have been found at heights up to 15,000 feet. They are much more solitary animals, frequently living high up in the trees, where they remain concealed during the day, emerging at night to feed. The cry of the tree hyrax is one of the most characteristic African sounds. When darkness has fallen, they utter an extremely piercing and long-drawn-out cry, which carries a great distance. It starts with a series of throaty croaking groans gradually rising to a crescendo and ultimately reaching the intensity of an unearthly high-pitched shriek which shatters the stillness of the night.

# Sirenians

Next to the whales, the sirenians have become more fully adapted to life in the oceans than any other group of mammals. Like the whales, their hind limbs have disappeared, and they never leave the water, even to give birth. But they are not related to the whales: their ancestry lies closer to the elephants and hyraxes.

The sirenian order contains only the dugong and three species of manatees. The order was at one time much larger. It included Steller's sea cow which attained a length of 24 feet, and which became extinct in 1768.

**Below**: Dugongs

The dugong is widely distributed in tropical seas where it inhabits shallow coastal waters, cropping the sea grass that is its principal food. It normally lives in pairs or small family groups, but large herds have occasionally been reported. The largest remaining dugong population is in Australian waters, notably along the coast of Queensland and off the southern coast of New Guinea.

The manatees live in certain of the coastal areas of the Caribbean, North and South America, and West Africa. Unlike the dugong they sometimes enter the larger rivers: one species is permanently established in fresh water in the Amazon river system. The silting-up of their coastal feeding grounds has caused manatees to disappear from some areas.

**Above**: Manatee

The sirenians are large, dull-witted, slow-moving animals with poor eyesight but good hearing. Because they live in shallow coastal waters and are completely defenceless, both dugongs and manatees are highly vulnerable to modern methods of hunting and fishing, and as the demand for their meat is unlimited, their numbers have been greatly reduced – a situation that is not helped by their low breeding rate.

# Odd-toed ungulates

This order contains the odd-toed hoofed mammals, that is to say mammals which normally have either one or three toes on each foot, with the weight of the body carried chiefly on the middle toe. This order is also characterized by the absence of antlers or horns – rhinoceros horn is not true horn but is made of closely packed hair-like fibres, and grows not from the skull but from the skin.

This once-large order is now represented by only six species of horses, wild asses and zebras; four species of tapirs; and five species of rhinoceroses. Nearly all of them are rare.

The tapirs are the only members of this order to inhabit the New World. Tapirs are stockily built animals standing about 3 feet tall and having a muzzle that has lengthened into a miniature trunk. Three of the four tapir species live in Central and South America, separated from the fourth in South East Asia by thousands of miles. Tapirs are creatures of the tropical forests; they are excellent swimmers, and often enter the water, partly to avoid being pestered by insects.

Water is essential to their existence, for which reason they must live close to lakes, swamps or rivers. They also require thick cover in which to hide by day. Tapirs are shy, retiring animals and are unable to tolerate disturbance. As their forested habitat is gradually cleared for farming and settlement they are forced to retreat into the wildest and most remote parts of their range.

Three of the five species of rhinoceroses live in Asia and two in Africa. The demand for

**Above**: Black rhinoceros

**Above**: Onager

**Below**: Malayan tapir

rhinoceros horn has resulted in the Asiatic species becoming very rare. The Javan rhinoceros in particular has been reduced almost to extinction: only about forty of them remain in Java's Udjung Kulon Reserve. The little hairy Sumatran rhino is almost as rare; and the great Indian rhinoceros numbers only about seven-hundred individual animals. In Africa, the black rhinoceros has fared better: although greatly reduced in numbers, it still occupies much of its natural range. The square-lipped rhinoceros, on the other hand, has almost disappeared from the northern part of its range, though it remains secure in the Umfolozi and Hluhluwe game reserves in Zululand.

Przewalski's horse is the only surviving species of wild horse. Until a century ago it roamed widely over the grasslands of Central Asia, but has been reduced almost to extinction. This border-land fringing the Gobi Desert is also the home of the Mongolian wild ass, or kulan, one of several varieties of wild ass widely distributed across Asia, from the intensely hot

**Below:** Przewalski's horse

**Below:** Zebras

deserts of Iran and India to the cold Tibetan plateau. The range of the wild ass extends into eastern Africa, where the last remaining herds are confined to the Horn of Africa.

The zebras are an exclusively African group of animals which, on the whole, have been more fortunate than the wild asses. The common zebra remains well distributed in Africa south of the Sahara; Grevy's zebra still exists (though in reduced numbers) in the arid parts of eastern Africa; the Cape mountain zebra is extremely rare; but Hartmann's mountain zebra from South West Africa and Angola – without doubt the finest of all the zebras – is holding its own.

43

# Even-toed ungulates

Even-toed ungulates differ from the preceding order by possessing two functional toes (each in the form of a horny hoof) on each foot to carry the weight of the body. Further differences include the presence in most species of horns or antlers, and much more complex stomachs which have the advantage of enabling

**Above**: Hippopotamus

**Below**: Sable antelope

them to swallow a great deal of green food quickly while the opportunity exists; later, at their leisure, by the process known as 'chewing the cud', they bring it back into their mouths a second time to be properly chewed.

This order, which is well represented in both the Old and the New Worlds, is divided into the following families: pigs, peccaries, hippopotamuses, camels, chevrotains, deer, giraffes, pronghorn, and bovids (cattle, sheep, goats, antelopes, gazelles, and duikers).

The hippopotamus is found only in Africa, where it occurs in most of the large lakes and rivers. Less than fifty years ago it was very common, but its numbers have been greatly reduced. Hippos are sociable animals, living in 'schools' of about a dozen animals but sometimes much larger ones. They spend most of the day resting and sleeping in the water, and are excellent swimmers. At dusk they go ashore to graze, often wandering a considerable distance from water. A much smaller species, the pygmy hippo, is found only in parts of West Africa where it lives in deep forest close to swamps and rivers, though it spends much less time in water than its bigger relative.

The camel has long been domesticated and used as a beast of burden, in which capacity it has been of enormous benefit to mankind. There are two camel species: the Arabian and the Bactrian. The Arabian camel is unknown in the wild state, but a few small herds of wild Bactrian camel still live on the fringes of the Gobi Desert in the same general area as the wild horse.

The camel family includes the llama, guanaco, alpaca and vicuna, all species found only in South America. Llamas and alpacas were domesticated and used as pack animals by the early pre-Inca civilizations and no longer exist in the wild state. But the guanaco and the vicuna survive in the wild, though both are becoming increasingly scarce. The vicuna, which lives high in the Andes, has the distinction of possessing the most valuable wool in the world.

The pronghorn is a purely North American animal. It is the only surviving member of its family and is unique because its horns are not permanent as with the antelopes but are shed every year like the antlers of a deer. The pronghorn is an inhabitant of the open plain, in particular of the great prairie-lands of western

**Above**: Red deer

**Above**: Bactrian camels

North America. Little more than a century ago the pronghorn population was estimated to total forty million. Only the huge herds of bison were more plentiful, but, like the bison, it has been reduced to a fraction of its former numbers. The pronghorn has a prominent rump patch of long white hairs which can be raised like a white fan as a warning signal.

45

Pronchorns

A similar 'fan', extending from the middle of the back to the tail, is also characteristic of the springbok. The lyre-horned springbok lives in South Africa, and derives its name from its habit of frequently springing high into the air: during these leaps, which normally take the animal about eight feet into the air, the white 'fan' is opened. Until the end of the last century the springbok herds occasionally undertook very spectacular migrations; literally millions of them assembled in massed herds and moved across country, allowing nothing to turn them from their course. These great 'treks' are however a phenomenon of the past which is unlikely ever to be repeated.

The giraffe is far taller than any other land animal. Its long neck gives it the advantage of reaching leaves that are too high for other hoofed animals. The giraffe is a creature of the plains: its only living relative, the okapi, is by contrast a resident of the dense equatorial forests. Giraffe live in small herds, but okapis live singly or in pairs. Both species have very short, skin-covered horns (though they are absent in the female okapi).

Among the many varieties of deer, the red deer is one of the most widely distributed in the woodlands of Europe and Asia. Its close relative, the wapiti, is a larger animal that lives in North America. The only deer to live in Africa is the Barbary stag, which lives in cork-oak forests along the frontier between Algeria and Tunisia. Very few remain: at last count the total was estimated at one hundred and fifty.

The fallow deer is distinguished by flattened antlers. This species came originally from the Middle East, but has been introduced into many parts of the world. Although now scarce in its homeland, it is a common resident of deer parks in Europe. A close relative, the Persian fallow deer, is however one of the rarest mammals in the world.

**Above**: Giraffe

46

# INDEX Page numbers in bold type refer to illustrations

**The illustrations in this book have been selected from the
Hamlyn all-colour paperbacks
ANIMALS OF AUSTRALIA AND NEW ZEALAND
by Richard Sadleir,
THE ANIMAL KINGDOM by Sali Money,
ANIMALS OF SOUTHERN ASIA by Michael Tweedie,
MAMMALS OF THE WORLD by Michael Boorer,
WILD CATS by Michael Boorer and
MONKEYS AND APES by Prue Napier**

Published 1973 by The Hamlyn Publishing Group Limited
London · New York · Sydney · Toronto
Hamlyn House, Feltham, Middlesex, England
© Copyright The Hamlyn Publishing Group Limited 1973
ISBN o 600 38061 o
Printed by Litografía A. Romero, S. A. Santa Cruz de Tenerife (Spain)